GW00402269

# BEST OF IRISH

## A CELEBRATION OF INCREDIBLE IRELAND

HANNAH MULHOLLAND

Michael O'Mara Books Limited

First published in Great Britain in 2009 by
Michael O'Mara Books Limited
9 Lion Yard
Tremadoc Road
London SW4 7NQ

A CIP catalogue record for this book is available from the British Library.

Papers used by Michael O'Mara Books Limited are natural, recyclable
products made from wood grown in sustainable forests. The manufacturing
processes conform to the environmental regulations of the country of origin.

ISBN: 978-1-84317-341-0

1 3 5 7 9 10 8 6 4 2

Designed and typeset by K DESIGN, Somerset

Printed and bound in Italy by L.E.G.O.

www.mombooks.com

# CONTENTS

# INTRODUCTION

For a tiny country at the farthest reaches of Western Europe, Ireland has made an incomparable impression on the wider world.

Wherever they travel, the Irish are warmly welcomed. But what is it about their home country that so captivates the imagination?

Is it its reputation as a mystical land of 'little people', white-washed cottages and distinctive 'characters'? Its rich musical and literary output? Its defiance and survival in the face of oppression? Or is it simply the renowned charm, wit and welcoming nature of Ireland's natives?

It may well be all of these things. In *Best of Irish*, I have drawn together Ireland's cultural tapestry, its sites of natural beauty and historical interest, and its most remarkable achievements, alongside its greatest ambassadors from politics, the arts and sciences – in a compendium that captures the best-loved aspects of this fascinating little nation.

HANNAH MULHOLLAND, 2009

# THE OLD COUNTRY

Staggeringly, it is estimated that for 70–80 million people across the globe, Ireland is 'the old country'.

**Emigrant Nation**
Ireland has seen its sons and daughters settle throughout Europe, primarily in England, France and Germany; journey to the far reaches of the southern hemisphere to put down roots in Australia and New Zealand; and make their home in Argentina, where Irish descendents, including the family of Che Guevara Lynch (1928–67), make up 3 per cent of the population.

As a result, Irish descendants now outnumber the population of the old country thirteen to one: not bad work for an island the same size and population as the state of Georgia.

## The Irish Pub

These figures might explain why every city worldwide seems to boast a selection of Irish-themed pubs.

Usually kitted out with retro signs for tobacco, Guinness and Jameson whiskey – alongside portraits of Ireland's most famous writers, playwrights and poets – the Irish pub is internationally renowned as an honest, no-frills hostelry that appeals to locals and tourists alike. The world over, everyone is having a crack at capturing the legendary 'craic'.

## Ireland and the White House

It is America, however, that boasts the largest and proudest descendant community, with almost 36 million US citizens reporting Irish ancestry.

Indeed, the very first president of the United States, George

Washington (1732–99), had a little green in his blood; and Ireland can claim more than twenty American presidents as near or distant relatives.

This impressive roll call of Irish-Americans includes Ulysses S. Grant, Theodore Roosevelt, Woodrow Wilson, Harry S. Truman, Lyndon B. Johnson, Richard Nixon, Jimmy Carter, Ronald Reagan, Bill Clinton and the Bushes, senior and junior.

Even President Barack Obama has Irish roots – his great-great-great-grandfather was a shoemaker from County Offaly.

## JFK

Yet no US president captured Irish hearts like John Fitzgerald Kennedy (1917–63).

In 1963, JFK visited the cottage in Dunganstown, Wexford, where his Kennedy kinfolk had lived before emigrating to America. There he uttered the immortal words: 'This is where it all began …' and Ireland swooned.

## Politics Aside

Naturally, Irish-Americans haven't just made an impact politically. The following famous folk all claimed Irish ancestry:

- James Cagney (actor)
- Walt Disney (animator)
- John Ford (film director)
- F. Scott Fitzgerald (novelist)
- Billy the Kid (outlaw)

## St Patrick's Day

With 12 per cent of the US population identifying as Irish-American, the country tops the charts for the biggest St Patrick's Day parades (in which even the rivers are dyed green), while Canada and Australia come a close second and third. England usually puts on a very good show, as does New Zealand.

## The Honorary Irish

Far from commemorating a Bible-wielding, snake-banishing former slave who may have converted a country (see page 12), St Patrick's Day is all about the Irish. Whether you can claim kinship or not, on 17 March each year – from Munich to Montserrat, Moscow to Mexico – everybody's Irish.

The oddest place to find St Patrick's Day celebrated? Montevideo, Uruguay, where the drinking-spinning-kissing games provide the best craic this side of Dublin.

## The Harp

The harp has represented Ireland for 1,000 years.

It was adopted as an emblem during the reign of High King (and harpist) Brian Boru (941–1014) in the eleventh century and later became popularized as a symbol of resistance, despite being part of the Royal Standard of English kings.

### Who Was St Patrick?

This is subject to debate, but two fifth-century figures are usually proposed as possible solutions.

First up is a Roman Briton living in Wales, who was kidnapped as a teen and brought to Ireland to serve as a slave. He escaped, but later returned as a missionary.

The other is Palladius, a Christian deacon from the Roman province of Gaul in Western Europe, who was thought to have been sent to Ireland by Pope Celestine.

Legend attributes St Patrick, Ireland's patron saint, with banishing snakes from the land (though arguably there were none there to begin with).

## The Shamrock

Instantly recognized as the symbol of
Ireland, the shamrock is a tiny three-
leafed clover said to bring good luck.

On St Patrick's Day, a small bouquet of
it is worn pinned to the lapel, as the story
goes that the saint used the plant to illustrate the
Blessed Trinity – each leaf representing the Father, Son
and Holy Spirit respectively.

Although the harp usually appears as Ireland's official
insignia, the shamrock is better known internationally.
It represents the nation's sports teams, and even makes an
appearance on the passport of Montserrat and the flag of
Montreal to acknowledge the large Irish presence in both
places.

'When the Irishman is found outside of Ireland in
another environment, he very often becomes a
respected man.'
James Joyce

**The Tricolour**

Like the Irish state, the tricolour flag is less than 100 years old. Well, that's not entirely true.

It was first introduced in 1848 by Irish nationalist and American Civil War general Thomas Meagher (1823–67) – but it wasn't hoisted on a flagpole until it fluttered above the General Post Office in Dublin during the short-lived Easter Rising of 1916 (see page 48).

The green of the flag represents Ireland's Gaelic tradition, while the orange stands for the supporters of William of Orange (see page 38) in the North. Finally, the white embodies peace between the two.

'Eternal is the fact that the human creature born in Ireland and brought up in its air is Irish. I have lived for twenty years in Ireland and for seventy-two in England; but the twenty came first, and in Britain I am still a foreigner and shall die one.'      George Bernard Shaw

# Mystical People,
# Mystical Places

**Fairies**

Fairies, or 'the little people', have had a place in Irish lore as long as popular memory can recall.

Many sinister acts – not least cursing, maiming or even killing – have been attributed to these mythical creatures, mainly against those who have trespassed on their land. Another favourite pastime is stealing human babies and replacing them with their own fairy changelings.

> 'Ireland's ruins are historic emotions surrendered to time.'
>
> Horace Sutton

# 'The Stolen Child'

Come away, O human child!
To the waters and the wild
With a faery, hand in hand,
For the world's more full of weeping than you can
    understand.

The work of the Irish poet W. B. Yeats (1865–1939; see
page 57), 'The Stolen Child' was written in 1886 and is
based on Irish legend.

Extracts from 'The Stolen Child' and 'The Lake Isle of Innisfree'
(page 58) by W. B. Yeats are reproduced by permission of A P Watt Ltd
on behalf of Gráinne Yeats.

## The Elfin Shoemaker

While the green ensemble, white stockings and Puritan-style hat are a recent addition, the legend of the leprechaun has been around in one form or another for thousands of years.

This elusive fellow loves nothing more than mischief and making sport of man's greedy nature. By trade he is a shoemaker, but is surprisingly rich and has his very own pot of gold to prove it.

This is to be forfeited to any human who can catch him – but few are up to the challenge.

## Connemara

Rugged, breathtaking and barren; lashed by the wild Atlantic; criss-crossed with rough-hewn stone walls: Connemara is home to some of the most fiercely independent and traditional people in the country.

Irish Gaelic (see page 32) remains the first language of many of the region's inhabitants, some of whom still farm the land and cut their own turf from the peat-rich bogs.

## The Banshee

Most people know the expression 'to scream (or wail) like a banshee', but few know anything about the mythical female figure making all the noise.

The banshee is seen as a foreteller of death. When her wail is heard outside a house, it spells doom for someone within.

The banshee has variously been depicted as a young woman or a hag. In both cases, she has long flowing hair, and eyes red from crying.

## Giant's Causeway

Combining the primeval with the folkloric, the breathtaking causeway has long been Northern Ireland's biggest tourist attraction.

Composed of geometric-looking basalt columns of varying heights – formed many millions of years ago by a volcanic eruption – it doesn't look quite of this earth. As such, it's small wonder that it comes with a mythical tale attached.

## The Causeway's Myth

Legend has it that the warrior Fionn mac Cumhaill (see page 23) built the Causeway so that he could walk across the sea to Scotland to do battle with his enemy Benandonner.

The fight never took place, however, due to the hugely proportioned Benandonner being frightened out of his wits by the relatively diminutive Fionn masquerading as a steak-eating baby. Assuming Fionn himself must be huge if this was his child, Benandonner fled, ripping up the Causeway so he couldn't be followed by mac Cumhaill.

## Glendalough

Glendalough is a place of extraordinary natural beauty. Set in a mountain valley in County Wicklow and sandwiched between the still waters of two lakes, Glendalough started life as a monastic settlement in the sixth century, under the auspices of the legendary St Kevin.

It features a number of well-preserved buildings, not least the stone gateway, the cathedral and the quaint St Kevin's Church or 'Kitchen'. Also still standing – at 30 metres tall – is the impressive round tower, originally built to protect the settlement from raiders.

## The Burren

The Burren in County Clare is a 250-square-kilometre area of incredible geological and archaeological richness. Its name comes from the Irish *boireann,* meaning 'great rock'.

A vast limestone plateau, the Burren doubles as a megalithic treasure trove, and features over ninety different sites, including the gravity-defying Poulnabrone portal dolmen (tomb) and the cliff-top Cahercommaun ring fort.

It's also littered with a bevy of world-class caves. The Burren's dramatic landscape is thought to inspire the distinctive traditional music of the nearby Doolin area, known as the 'West Clare Style'.

## Hill of Tara

Set on a glorious green plateau, with a view that on a clear day seems to capture the whole country, this prehistoric site is thought to have once been the seat of the High Kings of Ireland.

Tara features the earthwork remains of a number of ring forts and a banqueting hall. One of its better-preserved monuments is the remarkable Lia Fáil, a standing stone that is said to roar when touched by Ireland's rightful king.

If that wasn't enough, St Patrick himself is said to have visited Tara, and, in the early twentieth century, a group of British Israelites searched the site for the Ark of the Covenant.

## The Aran Islands

These, the last outposts of Europe, lie off the west coast of Connemara. Here, the ancient ways of life have been carefully preserved – as have the famous knitting patterns.

# THE BIRTH OF THE NATION

**Who are the Irish?**
Ireland's first inhabitants were Mesolithic hunter-gatherers from Continental Europe and Britain, who found their way to the Emerald Isle via Scotland and Wales some 8–10,000 years ago.

**The Story Begins ...**
Archaeological finds help to trace the development of life in Ireland through the millennia, but earthworks and standing stones only tell us so much. Mythology provides a more vivid picture of the early Irish.

Such stories feature ancient peoples known as the Fir Bolg, Tuatha De Danann, Gaels and Milesians – peoples who populated the land ... and then battled each other for control of it.

## Fionn mac Cumhaill

One of the best-known figures of Irish mythology, Fionn mac Cumhaill (whose name is often anglicized to Finn McCool) was the leader of a band of warriors known as the Fianna.

He features in many outlandish tales of heroism and adventure, including being credited with killing a fire-breathing fairy that terrorized Tara, and with building the Giant's Causeway (see page 18).

## The Celts

The term 'Celtic' covers a broad grouping of tribes originating from Central and Western Europe, bound together by a common language family. With the spread of the Roman Empire, the once-dominant Celts were pushed to the extreme west of the continent – to Brittany, Scotland, Wales … and Ireland.

Stories of Celtic ferocity in battle – with lime-stiffened hair, war paint and piercing cries – come primarily from Roman accounts. The Celts who first inhabited Ireland were in fact farmers. Albeit farmers who revered metalcraft, harp-playing and poetry.

## The Vikings and Normans

In the mid-tenth century AD, Scandinavian invaders known as Vikings took charge. By around 1169, however, the Normans were top dogs. Following many brutal battles, they took control of most of the country.

As the Vikings had done before them, the Normans integrated into Gaelic society: testament to this assimilation is the prevalence of Irish surnames with the Norman 'Fitz' prefix.

It's not for nothing that Ireland has the moniker 'the land of the thousand welcomes'.

# Ernest Shackleton

(1874–1922)

---

The intrepid Antarctic explorer Ernest Shackleton was born into a wealthy Anglo-Irish family from County Kildare and embarked on his first expedition in 1901, alongside Captain Scott (1868–1912) on the *Discovery*.

In all, Shackleton made four expeditions to the Antarctic, breaking the 'Farthest South' record twice. For his courage, he won international esteem, and a knighthood in 1909. He later gave talks on his harrowing and often death-defying experiences.

Perhaps the best known of these is the 1914–17 Imperial Trans-Antarctic Expedition, aboard the doomed *Endurance*. The ship was crushed by ice in the most inhospitable of territories – and yet Shackleton managed to guide its entire crew to safety.

In 2002, he was voted eleventh in the BBC's poll of the 100 Greatest Britons.

# A TASTE OF IRELAND

**Whiskey vs Whisky**

The Irish and the Scots have long been in competition over their whiskey-making prowess. The fact that the very word is derived from the Gaelic word for water ('*uisce*' or '*uisge*') attests to just how seriously both nations take the drink.

The Scots are certainly more prolific whisky (Scottish spelling) producers, but does that make them better? You'll have to let your taste buds decide.

In recent years, a third competitor has emerged to stake its claim as the finest whiskey-producing nation. It may seem unlikely, but that competitor is Japan.

## The Black Stuff

Next to the shamrock and the harp (see page 13), a black-and-white pint of Guinness is one of the most recognizable symbols of Ireland.

From its humble beginnings in 1759 under the auspices of fledgling brewer Arthur Guinness at a small site at St James's Gate in Dublin, the drink has become an international favourite: the famous stout is now brewed in forty countries and sold in 150.

## The Perfect Pint

Arguably, it is in its home country that the very best Guinness is served – maybe because Irish bartenders are endowed with the patience required to pour the perfect pint.

This is achieved by first pouring three quarters of the pint and then leaving it to sit for three minutes, before topping it off for a delicious creamy finish.

## Irish Stew

The Irish are known for their honest, hearty fare, the most famous example of which is perhaps Irish stew, which has been served up since at least 1800.

The dish's lengthy stewing time evolved for two reasons: the Irish tradition of open-fire cooking, and the frequent use of older mutton as the central ingredient. Sheep's wool and milk was often valued more highly than their meat, so by the time the elderly creatures came to the pot, they demanded hours of steady simmering.

### A Simple Irish Stew Recipe (serves four)

All you need to be able to make one of the country's most famous dishes.

### Ingredients:

4 lamb chops; 4 carrots (quartered); 4 onions (quartered); salt and pepper, to taste; 1 pint of lamb stock; 1 tbsp pearl barley; 4 floury potatoes (cut into rough chunks); 15g butter; 1 tbsp thyme; 1 tbsp parsley

**Method:**

1. Cut the fat off the chops and render it in a large, deep pan. Discard the solid pieces.
2. Toss the trimmed chops, and then the carrots and onions, in the rendered fat for several minutes.
3. Add the stock and sprinkle the pearl barley over the meat. Finally, put the potatoes on top, season, and simmer for at least two hours.
4. Skim any fat off the top of the dish, and then add the butter and herbs. Cook for a further five minutes, then serve immediately.

## The Potato

The potato was introduced to Ireland in the sixteenth century. Filling and easy to grow, it quickly became subsistence food for the poor Irish natives.

Though it no longer takes centre stage in the modern nation's diet, the potato is still a hugely popular staple.

### Irish Potato-Based Dishes

- A classic Irish potato dish is **colcannon**: made from mashed potato, kale or cabbage, and butter.
- Another variation on the theme, involving spring onions in place of cabbage, is **champ**.
- **Boxty** is a favourite too – it's a fried pancake made using both raw and mashed potato, flour, baking soda and buttermilk.

### Fancy a Tipple?

Food aside, potatoes have also been used to brew the infamous Irish moonshine known as *Poitín*.

It's a drink that requires a rather strong stomach: it's practically pure alcohol.

> 'Ah, Ireland ... That damnable, delightful country, where everything that is right is the opposite of what it ought to be.'
> Benjamin Disraeli

# THE GIFT OF THE GAB

### The Blarney Stone

Built into the parapet of a castle in County Cork and said to bestow the 'gift of the gab' upon those who kiss it, the Blarney Stone is an object swathed in mystery.

Some say the mystical stone was a gift from Scotland's Robert the Bruce. Others claim biblical origins: that it was struck by Moses to produce water for the fleeing Israelites or, alternatively, was used by Jacob as a pillow.

To kiss it, one must lie on the ground and dangle over the parapet. It's definitely not a feat for the faint-hearted, but if the legend is to be believed, one emerges as eloquent as the smoothest of Irishmen.

## The Irish Language

Known in Ireland as Gaeilge and to the rest of the world as Gaelic, the Irish language developed from that spoken by the Iron Age Celts.

The earliest written evidence of 'primitive' Irish is found in Ogham inscriptions from the fifth century. Not long afterwards, 'old' Irish began to appear in the margins and notes of Latin manuscripts written by native scholars.

## A Tongue for Modern Times

The language was eroded during the centuries of British rule. Today, it's the native tongue of between just 20,000 and 70,000 people, concentrated in Galway, Donegal and Kerry.

Constitutionally, Irish is the first language of the Republic and features frequently in officialdom.

'There is no language like the Irish for soothing and quieting.'
John Millington Synge

**'Amn't I Irish meself?' 'Is it Irish you are?'**

The influence of Gaelic upon the way that English is spoken in Ireland gives the language an inimitable charm.

This is sometimes reflected in sentence structure. For example, the question 'Is it Irish you are?' sounds fine to Irish ears, but might leave other English-speakers baffled.

Meanwhile, 'Amn't I?' is used as 'Am not I?', a peculiarly Irish variant of the standard English 'Aren't I?'

### Hiberno-English

Examples of Hiberno-English – that is, English as spoken by the Irish – are countless, but here are just a few:

- 'Come here to me', meaning 'Listen here'
- 'To give out' to someone, meaning 'to scold' them
- 'So', as in 'That's grand, so', meaning 'That's fine'
- 'Will' in place of 'shall', as in 'Will we go out tonight?'

33

And here are a few choice examples of colloquial Hiberno-English words:

| | |
|---|---|
| Bold | Naughty |
| Chiseler | Child |
| Deadly | Great, or cool |
| Eejit | Fool |
| Quare | Strange |
| Whisht | Be quiet |

'When anyone asks me about the Irish character, I say look at the trees. Maimed, stark and misshapen, but ferociously tenacious.'
Edna O'Brien

# IRELAND UNDER FIRE

Historically, Ireland has long been subject to invasions and oppression by occupying forces, and 'wars' between rival clans and would-be leaders.

This section digests the battle for autonomy – and, in 'An Independent Ireland' (see page 48), celebrates the independence that was achieved by the Irish people, against all the odds.

## Origins of the Struggle for Independence

The invasion of Ireland by the Normans in the twelfth century was the first phase in a long line of conquests by the rulers of Britain.

Their national grip soon contracted, however, to an area around Dublin known as 'the Pale'. Throughout history, this became famous as an English-controlled part of Ireland, and led to the expression 'beyond the pale', which is still in use today.

## A Right Royal To-Do

The next concerted effort to dominate the whole country came from Henry VIII (1491–1547). He insisted that Ireland be 'anglicized': that the Gaelic language and culture be abandoned and that Roman Catholicism be rejected outright.

The king stopped short of the extensive colonizing project recommended by his advisers, but his daughter, Elizabeth I (1533–1603), began the process of 'the plantation' during her reign, 'planting' English and later Scottish settlers across the country.

### Oliver Cromwell in Ireland

During the English Civil War (1642–51), rebels in Ireland seized the opportunity to regain power. They managed to reclaim much of the country and even established a government in Kilkenny.

In 1649, however, the newly inaugurated 'lord lieutenant and general for the parliament of England', Oliver Cromwell (1599–1658), landed with 3,000 battle-hardened troops to suppress Ireland's 'barbarous wretches'.

Such was the brutality of his forces that the country soon capitulated to English control once more. 'The curse of Cromwell be upon you' became an Irish oath that remained in use until the twentieth century.

## Battle of the Boyne (1690)

Having been dethroned in the bloodless revolution of 1688, Catholic King James II (1633–1701), former King of England and Scotland, used Ireland as a launching pad for his counter-attack on the throne, which was now held by his Dutch son-in-law, William of Orange (1650–1702).

James landed in a welcoming Ireland, quickly established a Catholic parliament and began reclaiming land from Protestant settlers, undermining William's rule.

The two men's next confrontation was far from bloodless: James's outmanned army made its last stand in 1690 on the banks of the River Boyne, not far from Drogheda. Defeated, James later died in exile; the dreams of a generation of Irish Catholics died with him.

To this day in Northern Ireland, the fraternal organization known as the Orange Order celebrates 'King Billy's' victory each July.

## The Rebellion of 1798

Inspired by the French Revolution, a group of Irish patriots headed by Theobold Wolfe Tone (1763–98) set up the Society of United Irishmen in 1791. Their goal: to establish an independent republic.

By 1797, the group had 100,000 members, as well as strong links with France.

In response to this threat, Ireland's governing powers introduced martial law, sparking a rebellion in Leinster and Ulster that lasted several months.

The conflict came to an end in October 1798 when the Royal Navy intercepted a French invasion led by Tone, resulting in heavy casualties, Tone's capture, and his death while awaiting execution.

> 'No man has a right to fix the boundary of the march of a nation; no man has a right to say to his country: "Thus far shalt thou go and no further."'
>
> Charles Stewart Parnell

# 'Amhran na bhFiann'

## ('The Soldier's Song')

Soldiers are we
Whose lives are pledged to Ireland
Some have come
From a land beyond the wave
Sworn to be free
No more our ancient sire land
Shall shelter the despot or the slave
Tonight we man the *bearna baol**
In Erin's cause, come woe or weal
'Mid cannon's roar and rifles' peal
We'll chant a soldier's song

* meaning 'gap of danger', this refers to an episode in the battle of New Ross during the 1798 rebellion

40

'Amhran na bhFiann' has been Ireland's national anthem since 1926.

Written by Peadar Kearney (1883–1942) and Patrick Heeney (1881–1911) in 1907 (and translated into Irish by Liam Ó Rinn [1888–1950] in 1923), it proved popular with Republicans and was sung during the 1916 Easter Rising (see page 48).

'Think – what have I got for Ireland? Something she has wanted these past seven hundred years. Will anyone be satisfied at the bargain? Will anyone? I tell you this – early this morning, I signed my death warrant. I thought at the time how odd, how ridiculous – a bullet may just as well have done the job five years ago.'

Michael Collins, December 1921, upon signing the peace treaty that ended the War of Independence

# Daniel O'Connell

(1775–1847)

---

Known as 'The Liberator' and 'The Emancipator', Daniel O'Connell is one of the great heroes of the Irish struggle for independence.

Born in Cahirciveen, County Kerry, O'Connell studied law in France, where popular ideas regarding equal rights are thought to have greatly influenced him.

A believer in non-violence, O'Connell set up the Catholic Association in 1823 to lobby for the right of Irish Catholics to become MPs. Three years later, the first pro-Catholic emancipation candidates won seats in parliament, and later the right to decline to swear the oath of supremacy.

O'Connell was unsuccessful in his final endeavour, however – to have the 1800 Act of Union, which bound Irish domestic matters to the British parliament, repealed.

# Charles Stewart Parnell

(1846–91)

---

Born into a well-connected Protestant family, Charles Stewart Parnell was an unlikely advocate of Irish nationalism.

He was elected to the House of Commons as a Home Rule League MP in 1875, and there set about obstructing the normal course of parliamentary business to draw attention to Irish issues and demand self-government for the country.

Parnell also became involved in the Land League, which sought to help poor tenant farmers and abolish landlordism, inspiring the downtrodden Irish to demand their rights as rent-payers and as citizens.

However, when his relationship with a married woman, Catherine 'Kitty' O'Shea, was exposed during her divorce trial, the scandal effectively ended his political career and he died not long afterwards, in 1891.

# THE GREAT FAMINE (1845–49)

The Famine was a watershed in Irish history and led to an intensification of the struggle against the country's British rulers and landlord classes.

## Famine Facts

In the mid-nineteenth century, a large proportion of Ireland's native population were poor tenant farmers, working tiny plots for their own subsistence and to furnish their landlords with exportable produce.

The potato was the main staple for a third of the population. When the entire crop failed due to blight in

1845 and 1846, countless families starved to death or died of diseases, like typhus, that appeared in the wake of the Famine.

The Famine lasted for four years and led to the death of approximately one million people – and the emigration of a further million to Britain and America.

### The Only Escape
With no meaningful aid from the ruling British government, those who could, left the country. Many flooded into Liverpool.

### The United States
Those journeying in the opposite direction, across the vast Atlantic to America, faced perilous conditions aboard vessels that became known as 'coffin ships' due to the huge number of passengers who died en route.

Gruesomely, it is said that sharks used to follow the boats in packs, as so many corpses were thrown overboard.

The mass exodus to America created a thousands-strong community that is today millions strong. In fact, it's six times the current population of Ireland itself.

## The Generosity of the Choctaw Tribe

Moved by stories from famine-stricken Ireland, the Native American Choctaw Tribe of Oklahoma collected $170 in aid in 1847, a considerable sum at the time.

The significance of this gesture cannot be underestimated. Only a few years earlier, the tribe's lands had been seized and it was forced to undertake a 500-mile hike along the aptly titled 'Trail of Tears': a harrowing journey that killed more than 10,000.

## Chief Robinson

A number of events commemorating the remarkable generosity of the Choctaws have been held in recent years.

In the early 1990s, the then President of Ireland, Mary Robinson, was made an honorary tribal chief.

# 'The Famine Song (Praties They Grow Small)'

This is a contemporary song from Ireland in the late 1840s (praties = potatoes, from the Irish Gaelic *prátaí*, plural of *práta*).

> Oh the praties they grow small, over here
> Oh the praties they grow small
> And way up in Donegal
> We eat them skins and all, over here, over here
> We eat them skins and all, over here.

# AN INDEPENDENT IRELAND

### Easter Rising 1916

In the middle of the First World War (1914–18), outside the General Post Office (GPO) in Dublin on Easter Monday 1916, a schoolteacher and poet named Patrick Pearse (1879–1916) read out a revolutionary document: 'The Proclamation of the Irish Republic'.

Though promised arms from Germany had failed to show up, his ragtag group of rebels decided to go ahead with their Rising and managed to take over a number of key buildings in the city.

## Ireland Responds

The rebels' gamble that their actions would stir the people of Ireland to join them did not pay off and the small group of insurgents faced the brute force of the British Army alone. They surrendered a few days later, by which time the GPO had been all but destroyed by shelling.

Although the nation had not responded to the initial battle cry, when fifteen of the men, including Pearse, were executed, the cause of independence took on a new and immediate importance across the land.

'People will say hard things of us now, but we shall be remembered by posterity and blessed by unborn generations.'
Patrick Pearse, two days before his execution

# James Connolly

## 1868–1916

---

Alongside Pearse, the much-revered James Connolly was a key leader of the 1916 rebellion.

Despite his poor background (his father had been a manure carter and his mother a domestic servant), Connolly was one of the leading Marxist theorists of the time and a hugely important figure in the Scottish and Irish trade union movements.

Raised in Edinburgh by Irish immigrant parents, Connolly joined the British Army at just fourteen, and was stationed in Ireland. There he saw at first hand the oppression of his people and made a decision to fight with and not against them.

Later, Connolly was in charge of the Dublin Brigade of the Irish Citizen Army and took the GPO during the 1916 Rising. After the surrender, he was so badly wounded that he was unable to stand for his execution on 12 May.

# 'James Connolly'

The spirit of freedom, they tried hard to quell
But above all the din, came the cry, 'No surrender!'
'Twas the voice of James Connolly, the Irish rebel.

From the traditional ballad, authorship unknown.

## The War of Independence (1919–21)

Lasting two and a half years, the War of Independence
was fought guerrilla-style against government forces by
the Irish Republican Army under Michael Collins (1890–
1922), and politically by the
newly established breakout
parliament, Dáil Éireann,
under Éamon de Valera
(1882–1975), and ultimately
led to the establishment of
the Irish Free State.

A truce was finally called on 11 July 1921. The leaders of the Irish parliament met their British counterparts to negotiate a peace treaty.

The result was an agreement that granted Ireland independence as the Irish Free State – albeit with serious restrictions, not least the continuation of British rule in the North.

## The Good Friday Agreement

Although British rule continued unchallenged until the late 1960s, thereafter, for nearly thirty long years, the Troubles – a war of guerrilla and terrorist tactics by sectarian groups – dominated the scene.

Finally, on 10 April 1998, with considerable help from American political figures (including Senator George Mitchell and President Bill Clinton), a peace deal known as the Good Friday Agreement was brokered. This agreement ultimately paved the way for today's historic power-sharing government in Northern Ireland.

Key figures David Trimble and John Hume, a Unionist and a Republican respectively, were awarded the 1998 Nobel Peace Prize for their efforts in the negotiations.

'Two major political traditions share the island of Ireland. We are destined by history to live side by side. Two representatives of these political traditions stand here today. We do so in shared fellowship and a shared determination to make Ireland, after the hardship and pain of many years, a true and enduring symbol of peace.'
John Hume, in his Nobel Lecture, 10 December 1998

'Self-government is our right, a thing born in us at our birth, a thing no more to be doled out to us, or withheld from us by another people than the right to life itself — than the right to feel the sun, or smell the flowers, or to love our kind.'                    Roger Casement

# STORYTELLING

The literary achievements of the Irish seem almost disproportionate to the size of the country. It has a rich history of poetry, theatre and fiction, and today the Irish literati are still out in force on bookshop shelves, while scooping the top writing gongs.

## Once Upon a Time …
Known as 'the land of saints and scholars', Ireland was a hub of monastic learning and artistry during the Early Middle Ages.

No single artefact captures the spirit of this religious age better than that magnificent eighth-century tome, the Book of Kells.

## Book of Kells

Named for the monastery in County Meath in which it spent centuries of its life, this elaborately illuminated manuscript is chiefly comprised of the four gospels of the New Testament.

The artwork has become intrinsically linked with the idea of a 'Celtic' style – stunningly intricate knotwork, swirling patterns and animal motifs in striking colours, including gold.

The book is now reverentially housed in Trinity College, Dublin (see page 73), and is one of the capital's most popular attractions.

## The *Seanchaí*

The art of storytelling is much-prized by the Irish and until recently the *seanchaí* (storyteller) occupied a central role in the country's culture.

Traditionally, a *seanchaí* was a master wordsmith who made a living from his well-honed renditions, from memory, of an array of stories. Living an itinerant existence, the *seanchaí* would travel from village to village, sharing his tall tales with rapt audiences in exchange for food and shelter.

There are still a few people determined to keep this art alive, and it's not unusual to find a modern-day *seanchaí* entertaining a delighted hearthside group at one of the country's traditional festivals.

## A New Wave of Writers

The roll call of Ireland's contemporary talent includes John Banville, Anne Enright and Roddy Doyle, all of whom have won the Booker Prize in recent years.

Then, of course, there is that Irish-female-dominated genre, affectionately known as 'chick lit', in which the likes of Maeve Binchy, Marian Keyes and, recently, Cecelia Ahern have come to command the bestseller lists.

# William Butler Yeats

(1865–1939)

No figure looms larger in Irish literature than the poet, playwright and folklorist W. B. Yeats.

Yeats was born into a highly artistic family – both his father and his younger brother were painters, while William himself began writing poetry at an early age.

His interests in Irish folklore and storytelling led him to become one of the key figures in the Irish Literary Revival at the turn of the century. He was also instrumental in the establishment of the Abbey, Ireland's national theatre, which opened in 1904.

Yeats wrote several volumes of highly acclaimed poetry, for which he was rewarded with the Nobel Prize in Literature in 1923. He is also known to have dabbled in the occult and was a regular attendee at seances.

# 'The Lake Isle of Innisfree'

I will arise and go now, and go to Innisfree,
And a small cabin build there, of clay and
    wattles made:
Nine bean-rows will I have there, a hive for the
    honey-bee;
And live alone in the bee-loud glade.

'The Lake Isle of Innisfree' was first published in 1893 in
*The Rose*, Yeats's second volume of poetry. Showcasing
his early lyric style, it evokes the countryside of County
Sligo.

> 'We Irish are too poetical to be poets; we are a nation
> of brilliant failures, but we are the greatest talkers since
> the Greeks.'
> Oscar Wilde

## Literary Ireland

Irish artists have long had a profound influence on literature. Experimenters like Samuel Beckett (1906–89) and James Joyce (1882–1941) took, respectively, theatre and the novel in strange new directions.

Meanwhile, satirists such as Jonathan Swift (1667–1745) exposed the cruel oppression of the Irish with wit and pitiless purpose. In Swift's *Modest Proposal* (1729), he recommended that the Irish eat their young to stave off hunger:

> A young healthy child well nursed is at a year a most delicious, nourishing, and wholesome food, whether stewed, roasted, baked, or boiled.

Later, his fellow satirist George Bernard Shaw (1856–1950) produced incisive comedic plays attacking society's ills, while Oscar Wilde (1854–1900) subtly savaged the manners and mannerisms of the upper classes.

# Oscar Wilde

(1854–1900)

———————

Born into a wealthy Dublin family, Oscar Wilde enjoyed fame and infamy in equal portions during his brief life.

At the height of his career, having written plays such as *An Ideal Husband* and *The Importance of Being Earnest* (both 1895), Wilde was the toast of London's theatrical society, but towards the end of his life, he was disgraced and imprisoned for homosexual practices, then a crime.

The playwright, novelist and poet is best remembered for his scathing depictions of the English upper classes, whose frivolities were illustrated so wonderfully in his delicious satires.

Wilde's works continue to find new and adoring audiences, generation after generation.

## The Limerick

OK, so the limerick isn't actually from Limerick, nor is it even Irish. It was an Englishman, Edward Lear, who popularized the form. But sometimes you have to take a well-earned break from all the lofty stuff ...

NB: 'Dun Laoghaire' has the unlikely pronunciation 'Dun Leary'; 'youse' is slang for 'you', plural.

> There once was a lass from Dun Laoghaire
> Who'd drink and get stupidly teary.
> 'It'sh not from the booze,
> I'm jusht moved to see youse ...'
> – Which was rather a tenuous theory.

---

'That's the Irish people all over – they treat a joke as a serious thing, and a serious thing as a joke.'

Sean O'Casey, *The Shadow of a Gunman* (1923)

---

# Seamus Heaney

(1939–)

---

One of today's best-known poets, Seamus Heaney was born in a rural area between Counties Antrim and Derry in Northern Ireland in 1939.

Heaney published his first volume of poetry, *Death of a Naturalist*, in 1965 and worked as a teacher throughout the 1970s, before taking a position at Harvard in 1980. A few years later, he was elected Professor of Poetry at the University of Oxford and in 1995 was recognized with the highest honour of them all – the Nobel Prize in Literature.

He published his T. S. Eliot Prize-winning collection *District and Circle* in April 2006, but suffered a stroke later that year. Heaney currently lives in Dublin with his wife, the writer Marie Devlin.

# James Joyce

(1882–1941)

---

Dubliner James Joyce was born into a once well-to-do family, impoverished by a heavy-drinking father, in 1882.

Joyce had a love–hate relationship with the nation of his birth, and spent most of his life living abroad to escape what he perceived as the country's small-mindedness. Yet Ireland (and Dublin in particular) always took centre stage in his writing.

Joyce eloped to Zurich in 1904 with his lover Nora Barnacle and would never again live in Ireland. The couple had two children together and eventually married in 1931.

Though Joyce published only a handful of books – including *Dubliners* (1914), *A Portrait of the Artist as a Young Man* (1916), *Ulysses* (1922) and *Finnegans Wake* (1939) – and a small amount of poetry, his impact on modern literature has been incalculable.

# SOUNDS IRISH

**Enduring Traditions**

Irish traditional music takes many forms. Best known, perhaps, are its energetic jigs and reels, but there are a whole host of other styles and sounds to be heard, including those of a plaintive harp, a ceilidh band, or the haunting strains of Sean-nós (old-style) singing.

Irish music comes with its own distinctive range of instruments, too:

- the oileann pipes (akin to the bagpipes, but pumped)
- the bodhran (a drum played using both ends of one stick)

- the feadan (tin whistle)
- the fiddle (a violin with a funny name)

And then, of course, there's the dancing: ceilidh dancing, set dancing, step dancing (think *Riverdance* – see page 68), Sean-nós dancing … *and* there's a different outfit to go with each style of dance.

# 'The Rose of Tralee'

She was lovely and fair as the rose of the summer,
Yet 'twas not her beauty alone that won me;
Oh no, 'twas the truth in her eyes ever dawning,
That made me love Mary, the Rose of Tralee.

From the traditional nineteenth-century folk song.
The authorship is disputed; many attribute it to William Pembroke Mulchinock (1820–64).

## Brand Ireland

Artists from the Emerald Isle enjoy huge international followings, especially those who have a certain 'Irish' sound. The four-sibling group The Corrs combine traditional instruments like the fiddle and tin whistle with pop music, and have garnered massive fan bases in America and England, where their albums have been certified gold and platinum.

Sinead O'Connor also has a lilt that is undeniably Irish, though her music is more experimental in style. Brand Ireland's ultimate musical spokeswoman, however, has to be Enya.

## Enya

Formerly of the family folk group Clannad, Eithne (pronounced Enya) Ní Bhraonáin's ambient, mysticism-drenched albums evoke images of fairy queens, Celtic warriors and magical landscapes ... and sell by the tens of millions.

## Boy Bands

Another of Ireland's massive musical exports is the boy band. It's not that the Irish invented the format – just that they perfected it with groups like Boyzone and Westlife.

Carefully developed by manager Louis Walsh, both bands dominated the charts in their respective primes, with gentle love songs to melt their (mainly female) fans' hearts.

Always polite and immaculately turned out, these lads have a safe, boy-next-door charm that's more hot drink than hot date. Ireland hasn't produced many musical heartthrobs, sadly – unless you count the Argyll-sweater-wearing Daniel O'Donnell, of course.

## Eurovision

Perhaps the real proof of the international appeal of Ireland's music is its Eurovision record: the country heads the leader board with a total of seven wins since the competition launched in 1956.

The winning songs:

'All Kinds of Everything (Dana, 1970)

'What's Another Year?' (Johnny Logan, 1980)

'Hold Me Now' (Johnny Logan, 1987)

'Why Me?' (Linda Martin, 1992)

'In Your Eyes' (Niamh Kavanagh, 1993)

'Rock 'n' Roll Kids'
(Paul Harrington and Charlie McGettigan, 1994)

'The Voice' (Eimear Quinn, 1996)

Probably the most remarkable Eurovision story is that of Johnny Logan. He has won the competition an unmatched three times: as a singer, singer-songwriter and finally songwriter (he penned the 1992 entry).

And no one could forget 1994's *Riverdance* – the Eurovision interval performance that became a global stage sensation, and launched the career of one silk-shirt-wearing Michael Flatley.

## Strawberry Fields Forever

In all seriousness, Ireland has produced some phenomenal musical talent. It can even lay claim to half the Beatles – both Lennon and McCartney are of Irish descent.

## U2

However, the country's most successful and best-known musical export is, beyond question, U2. These four Dublin lads have been producing pop-rock gold for three decades: to date, they've won twenty-two Grammy Awards and sold over 140 million albums worldwide.

They've made a name for themselves in other ways too, not least their charity work and activism.

## Bono

U2's wraparound-shades-wearing, leather-clad front man, Bono, is a household name ... pretty much everywhere.

Born Paul Hewson in 1960 in Glasnevin, Dublin, Bono has stood beside many formidable world leaders to demand debt relief for the Third World and support for HIV/AIDS treatment.

# Bob Geldof

(1951–)

---

Providing Bono with some serious competition in the Mr Wonderful stakes, Dun Laoghaire-born (Sir) Bob Geldof first made his name with the Boomtown Rats back in the 1970s with the song 'I Don't Like Mondays'.

His work on 1985's Live Aid, the biggest charity concert the world has ever seen, brought hunger in Ethiopia and elsewhere in Africa to the world stage – literally. It raised over £150 million for famine relief, and Geldof was later knighted.

In July 2005, Geldof and his fellow Live Aid organizer Midge Ure staged Live 8, which consisted of ten free concerts across the world, held to raise awareness of the issues of poverty and debt in Africa.

# DUBLIN

The most common translation of the Irish capital's name into Gaelic today is *Baile Átha Cliath*, meaning 'the settlement of the ford of the reed hurdles (or wattles)'.

The name 'Dublin', however, is a direct derivative of *Dubh linn*, meaning 'black pool'.

Ireland's other cities are:

- Cork
- Galway
- Waterford
- Limerick
- Belfast (see page 92)

## Past and Present

As a settlement, Dublin is over 1,000 years old. It was established and later walled-in by Viking invaders in the late tenth century. Parts of those original walls still stand on the outskirts of Temple Bar in the city centre, near Wood Quay.

Following the Norman invasion in the twelfth century, Dublin became the administrative centre of the whole country and remains so to this day.

## Georgian Dublin

A building boom in the late seventeenth and early eighteenth centuries saw the construction of some of the city's most distinctive residential houses and squares.

The Georgian style was imported from England, but perfected in Dublin, where the houses were grander in scale to reflect the bulging purses of their ostentatious owners.

## Merrion Square

Among the city's five impressive Georgian squares, Merrion Square on the south side of the River Liffey is perhaps the most beloved.

Its former famous residents include Oscar Wilde's family, while its west side boasts Leinster House – the erstwhile Dublin domicile of the Earls of Kildare, now home to the Irish parliament – and the National Gallery of Ireland.

## Trinity College

Perhaps one of Dublin's best-known landmarks, Trinity College was founded in 1592 by Queen Elizabeth I and counts Jonathan Swift, Oscar Wilde (see page 60), Samuel Beckett, Bram Stoker and Ernest Walton (see page 74) among its graduates.

Covering a forty-seven-acre site in the heart of Dublin's city centre, the sprawling campus features a number of impressive buildings from different periods, including the Examination Hall, the chapel, and the Long Room in the library, which is home to the Book of Kells (see page 55).

# Ernest Walton

(1903–95)

---

The only Irishman to win the Nobel Prize in science, the physicist Ernest Walton is credited, alongside his work partner John Cockcroft, with 'splitting the atom'.

Born in Abbeyside, County Waterford, young Ernest's exceptional talents in maths and science won him a scholarship to study at Trinity College, Dublin, in 1922. He subsequently accepted a research post at Trinity College, Cambridge and there earned his PhD and met Cockcroft.

In 1932, Walton and Cockcroft successfully built a device capable of splitting the nuclei of lithium atoms. They were eventually rewarded for their work with the Nobel Prize in Physics in 1951.

## Christ Church Cathedral

Christ Church is the elder of Dublin's two magnificent medieval cathedrals. It was built in the early eleventh century under the auspices of the Viking king, Sitric Silkenbeard.

The cathedral's atmospheric crypt is the largest of its kind in Ireland and Britain, while the mummified 'Cat and Mouse' group, found perfectly preserved behind the organ some years ago, is eerily on display by the Choir.

## St Patrick's Cathedral

St Patrick's Cathedral is considerably larger than Christ Church – in fact, it's the largest church in Ireland.

It is claimed that the expression 'to chance your arm' (to take a risk) originated there. The story goes that in 1492, Gerald, Earl of Kildare cut a hole in one of its doors and thrust his arm through in an effort to call a truce with his enemy, James, Earl of Ormond. Luckily, Gerald's arm was spared.

## Symbols of Dublin

Dubliners have long had a habit of affixing unflattering rhyming names to new sculptural or public works that appear in the city. Here are a few examples:

'**The Hags with the Bags**' is a sculpture of two chatting women on a bench, which sits on the north side of the Ha'penny Bridge across the River Liffey from Temple Bar.

'**The Stiletto in the Ghetto**' is the latest Dublin monument to get the nickname treatment. A 120-metre-tall, needle-like structure that stands in the middle of O'Connell Street, it also goes by the names 'The Nail in the Pale' and 'The Stiffy by the Liffey'.

'It's not that the Irish are cynical. It's rather that they have a wonderful lack of respect for everything and everybody.'
Brendan Behan

**'The Floozy in the Jacuzzi'** – though she currently resides in storage, the Anna Livia fountain was once a central feature on O'Connell Street. (Anna Livia Plurabelle is a character in James Joyce's *Finnegans Wake* – see page 63.) Ending up as a watery rubbish bin, the fountain also had the monikers 'The Hoor in the Sewer', 'The Bitch in the Ditch' and 'The Damp Tramp'.

**'The Tart with the Cart'** – the statue of Molly Malone by sculptor Jeanne Rynhart. Molly stands at the top of Grafton Street and, over the years, has earned the names 'The Dolly with the Trolley', 'The Trollop with the Scallop' and, more kindly, 'The Dish with the Fish'.

'I think being a woman is like being Irish ... Everyone says you're important and nice, but you take second place all the same.'
Iris Murdoch

# 'Molly Malone'

In Dublin's fair city, where the girls are so pretty
I first set my eyes on sweet Molly Malone
As she wheeled her wheelbarrow through streets
   broad and narrow
Crying cockles and mussels alive alive O!

Alive alive O! Alive alive O!
Crying cockles and mussels alive alive O!

'Molly Malone' was first published in 1884, its authorship
attributed to composer James Yorkston. It has since
become Dublin's unofficial anthem.

# Robert Boyle

(1627–91)

───────────────

Hailed as the father of modern chemistry, Robert
Boyle was a gentleman scientist, theologian,
alchemist and inventor – and the fourteenth child of
Richard Boyle, the first Earl of Cork.

In his twenties, Robert became involved with a group
of thinkers and experimenters calling themselves the
'Invisible College'. Soon after, he began work on his
famous air pump and in 1662 devised what is now
known as Boyle's Law – that the volume of gas varies
inversely to its pressure.

The previous year, his book *The Sceptical Chymist*
(1661) came out, and is still viewed to this day as a
seminal text in the field of chemistry.

# SPORTING IRELAND

With nearly a sixth of its population being members of
the Gaelic Athletic Association (GAA), it's safe to say that
Ireland is a country that likes its home-grown sports.
These are:

- **Hurling**
  Not for the faint-hearted, this ancient Gaelic sport is
  played with axe-shaped sticks called 'hurleys' and a
  small, hard leather ball called a 'sliotar'.

  It is considered to be the world's fastest team sport
  and sticks can be swung any which way, so protective
  headgear is highly recommended.

- **Camogie**
  This game is very similar to hurling and is played by women. The primary difference is that players can hand-pass to score a goal.

- **Gaelic Football**
  Played with a slightly heavier ball than in soccer, this sport allows players to use their hands as well as feet to score and pass the ball. It also permits tackling of a more robust variety.

  Australian Rules football is perhaps its closest known cousin.

## Rugby

Though historically considered to be an 'English' sport and associated with the Anglo-Irish class, rugby has become a hugely popular sport in Ireland in recent years, helped considerably by the quality of the players on successive national teams.

Its all-time highest try scorer is its current captain Brian O'Driscoll; he is also considered by many to be among the best players in the world. Joining O'Driscoll on today's team is Ronan O'Gara, Ireland's highest overall point scorer in history.

## Soccer

Like much of the world, the sports-mad Irish are rather partial to soccer too. Ireland has produced some fine players over the years: its hall of fame includes George Best, Roy Keane and Robbie Keane.

Nationally, the Irish team were at their peak in the late 1980s and early 1990s. Under the stewardship of English legend Jack Charlton, they qualified for the World Cup for the first time in history.

'Jackie's Army' consisted of players like John Aldridge, Ronnie Whelan, Pat Bonner, Mark Lawrenson and Paul McGrath.

# Paul McGrath

(1959–)

One of the longest serving members of the Irish national football team, Paul McGrath is among the country's best-loved sports personalities.

McGrath was the 'illegitimate' child of an Irish mother and Nigerian father, and spent his childhood in Dublin orphanages.

After a brief stint as a security guard and sheet metal worker, McGrath began his football career with Dublin's St Patrick's Athletic in 1981. It wasn't long before he was beckoned to the UK to play for Manchester United, then Aston Villa (where he was known as 'God'), and ultimately Sheffield United.

McGrath had a long battle with alcoholism, which he details with characteristic honesty in his bestselling autobiography *Back from the Brink* (2006).

# Sonia O'Sullivan

(1969–)

Without doubt Ireland's most successful athlete, runner Sonia O'Sullivan has won six gold medals.* Though an Olympic gold always eluded her, she did take silver at the 2000 Games in Sydney.

Hailing from Cobh, County Cork, Sonia began her career in the late 1980s. Not content to represent just one country, in 2006 Sonia applied for dual citizenship so she could run for Australia in the Commonwealth Games in Melbourne. Unfortunately, injury prevented her from participating.

It's been some time since she last competed in a major athletic event, though she remains active in smaller events and is a multiple marathon winner.

* Three in the European Championships, one in the World Championships, and two in the World Cross-Country Championships.

## Golf

The sport in which Ireland performs best on the international stage is golf.

Prominent Irish golfers include Philip Walton and Paul McGinley, who coincidentally attended the same secondary school as Pádraig Harrington (see below) in the Dublin suburb of Rathfarnham.

Golf courses are something that the Irish do rather well. Locations like the K Club in Kildare and Druid's Glen in Wicklow are globally renowned.

## Pádraig Harrington

To date, the country's biggest golf success story is Pádraig Harrington.

Harrington was born in Dublin in 1971, the son of a Gaelic football star. Recently, he has racked up a number of impressive wins, including the Open Championship in 2007 and 2008 and the PGA Championship in 2008 – presenting Tiger Woods with some serious competition.

# IRELAND ON SCREEN

## Irish Television
Though the Irish are renowned for their wit, quality home-grown comedy was for years conspicuously absent from Ireland's TV schedules – that is, until the arrival of a certain sacrilegious satire …

## *Father Ted*
Casting the comic spotlight on the once untouchable profession of the priesthood, *Father Ted* follows the exploits of a put-upon and rather inept priest, Ted Crilly, who has been stationed on a remote island off the west coast of Ireland.

Created by Graham Linehan and Arthur Mathews, it proved an instant success, and became the launch pad for a host of Irish talent in the late 1990s, including stand-ups like Ardal O'Hanlon and Graham Norton. The show clinched two BAFTAs for Best Comedy Series, as well as a number of coveted British Comedy Awards.

## Stage 'Oirish'

On the big screen, Ireland has frequently been cast as an ultra-quaint land populated by a variety of clichéd characters.

In movies like *Darby O'Gill and the Little People* (1959), starring Sean Connery, the freckle-faced, garden gnome-style leprechauns are out in force. While in other films, such as *The Quiet Man* (1952), which features John Wayne as an American coming home to Ireland to find his roots, the natives are cast as a bunch of hard-drinking, lovable rogues, who like nothing better than a funeral and a fistfight.

In early Hollywood movies, Irish characters often show up as either drunks or policemen – or both.

## Contemporary Irish Cinema

Throughout the 1990s and 2000s, a number of hugely successful Irish films were released, including *The Commitments* (1991) and the Oscar-winning romance *Once* (2007), both starring musician Glen Hansard, and *Intermission* (2003) and *In Bruges* (2008), both starring Colin Farrell.

Meanwhile, Hollywood's love affair with Ireland continued with big-name actors queuing up to try out their brogues – with rather mixed results. Remember the following?

- Tom Cruise in *Far and Away* (1992)
- Brad Pitt in *The Devil's Own* (1997)
- Leonardo DiCaprio in *Gangs of New York* (2002)

---

'Ireland is a great country to die or be married in.'

Elizabeth Bowen

---

### *The Crying Game* (1992)

Winner of the Best Screenplay Oscar in 1993, Neil Jordan's *The Crying Game* is definitely one of the most talked-about Irish films of recent years.

Starring Stephen Rea as Fergus, an IRA volunteer, the film was praised for its sensitive portrayal of those caught up in the Troubles in Northern Ireland, from both the Irish and British perspective.

Fergus forms an unlikely bond with a captured British soldier, who makes him promise to look after his girlfriend, Dil, in London. When Fergus begins to fall for Dil, he discovers that she has a rather shocking secret … in a twist that kept audiences talking long after the credits stopped rolling.

# Jim Sheridan

(1949–)

---

Dublin-born writer and director Jim Sheridan made his name in 1989 with *My Left Foot*, his Oscar-winning biopic of disabled writer and artist Christie Brown (played by Daniel Day-Lewis).

Unashamedly nationalist in his politics, Sheridan has courted controversy with his compelling trilogy of Troubles films: *In the Name of the Father* (1993), *Some Mother's Son* (1996, writer) and *The Boxer* (1997).

Sheridan has received six Oscar nominations to date and won twenty-one international awards in the course of his stellar career.

---

'What you may take for lying in an Irishman is only his attempt to put an herbaceous border on stark reality.'

Oliver St John Gogarty

## Leading Men

When it comes to producing dishy leading men, Ireland tops the leader board. But who is the biggest heart-throb of them all?

If your criterion is 'rugged but charming', Liam Neeson and Gabriel Byrne are joint contenders. For smooth, classic good looks and that certain smouldering something, look no further than Daniel Day-Lewis and Pierce 'James Bond' Brosnan.

Then, of course, there are the downright beautiful leading men in the form of Jonathan Rhys Meyers and the perfect cheekbones of Cillian Murphy.

However, most will probably agree that it's not because of his acting skills that Colin Farrell is box-office gold.

> 'Ireland is where strange tales begin and happy endings are possible.'
> Charles Haughey

# BELFAST

The name 'Belfast' is an anglicized version of the Gaelic name '*Béal Feirste*', meaning 'Mouth of the River Farset'.

### In the Beginning
The site upon which the city was built is thought to have been inhabited since at least the Bronze Age.

Indeed, a 5,000-year-old henge known as the Giant's Ring lies close to Belfast's borders.

### King of the Castles
In the early twelfth century, Norman knight John De Courcy built two castles: one on what is now known, aptly enough, as Castle Street in the city centre, and a larger one to the north of the city, in Carrickfergus.

Only the latter castle still stands to this day, but both were massively important in terms of the development of Belfast as a bustling medieval town.

## In the Money
By the nineteenth century, Belfast had developed into a hub of industry, with linen, tobacco and ship-building as its key businesses.

Many grand buildings appeared at the time to reflect this prosperity, such as the elaborate neo-classical City Hall.

## City Hall
Set at the heart of Belfast, this edifice looks out on to the grand expanse of Donegall Square. Building work began in the late nineteenth century – shortly after Queen Victoria granted Belfast city status – and was completed in 1906.

Its towers and dome dominate the city skyline, while its interior boasts expanses of marble and stunning stained-glass features.

## Stormont

The seat of the Northern Ireland Assembly, Stormont was opened in 1932 to house the parliament set up after the Home Rule Bill of 1920.

The original plans for the building had to be toned down following the 1929 Wall Street Crash, but the resulting edifice is nonetheless hugely impressive, if not a little imposing.

## The Past One Hundred Years

The twentieth century was altogether a tough time for Belfast: the city was badly hit during the Blitz of the Second World War and later ravaged during the Troubles of the late 1960s to 1990s.

A massive rejuvenation project has injected new life into the city in recent years. Today, its formerly sparsely inhabited centre is thriving as never before.

---

'I'm Irish. We think sideways.'                     Spike Milligan

---

# MODERN IRELAND

Change has occurred in nearly every walk of Irish life in recent years.

The once poor cousin of Europe became one of her most buoyant economies (the infamous 'Celtic Tiger'); a people who expected little more than subsistence wages have become aspirational; and even the country's topography has shifted, with new towns popping up and existing ones stretching out to welcome waves of immigrants for the first time in many years.

Ireland has never been a more vibrant or exciting (or expensive) place to visit and reside. Yet despite the rapid pace of change, it retains much of its old-style charm.

The Irish are a people of many contradictions: rebels

and reactionaries who are religiously conservative; a once insular population that has produced poets and playwrights whose insights into human nature still dazzle; a pacifist nation that loves nothing better than dishing out a good verbal battering.

They are endlessly fascinated by themselves – and so they should be. It was not for nothing that Sigmund Freud said: 'This is one race of people for whom psychoanalysis is of no use whatsoever.'

Nor for nothing that the novelist Elizabeth Bowen once asked, 'Where would the Irish be without someone to be Irish at?'

'In Ireland, the inevitable never happens and the unexpected constantly occurs.'    Sir John Pentland Mahaffy